My SuperFather

A Christian children's rhyming book celebrating fathers from a biblical point of view

Copyrights

www.gnmkids.com

This book belongs to:

....

....

In the Bible we read of men, bold and true
Who loved God the Father as they chose to do
All that He asked, and so now we can see
The examples they left us for how life should be.

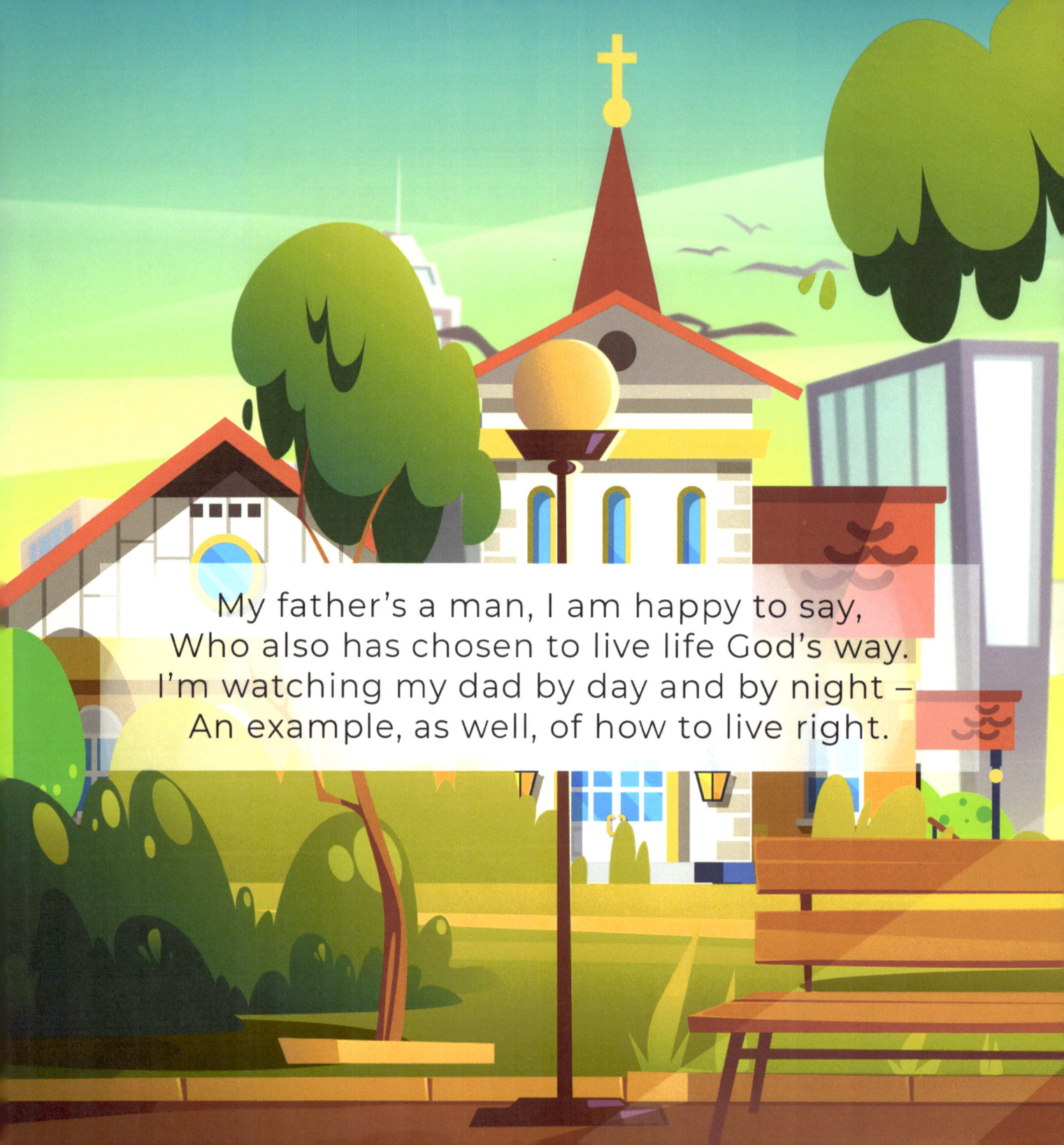

My father's a man, I am happy to say,
Who also has chosen to live life God's way.
I'm watching my dad by day and by night –
An example, as well, of how to live right.

Have you heard of ABRAHAM? He made the choice
To obey the Lord's will, when he heard His voice.
Though God gave Abraham difficult tasks,
He said, "I will do whatever God asks."
God made him the father of His chosen nation;
Through him, Christ was born and brought us salvation.

My dad reads his Bible and prays every day,
Like Abraham, seeking to live the Lord's way.

Do you know about DAVID? He made some mistakes,
But David declared, "I'll do what it takes
To return to the Lord and I'll try to live right,
The way that I should In the Lord's holy sight."

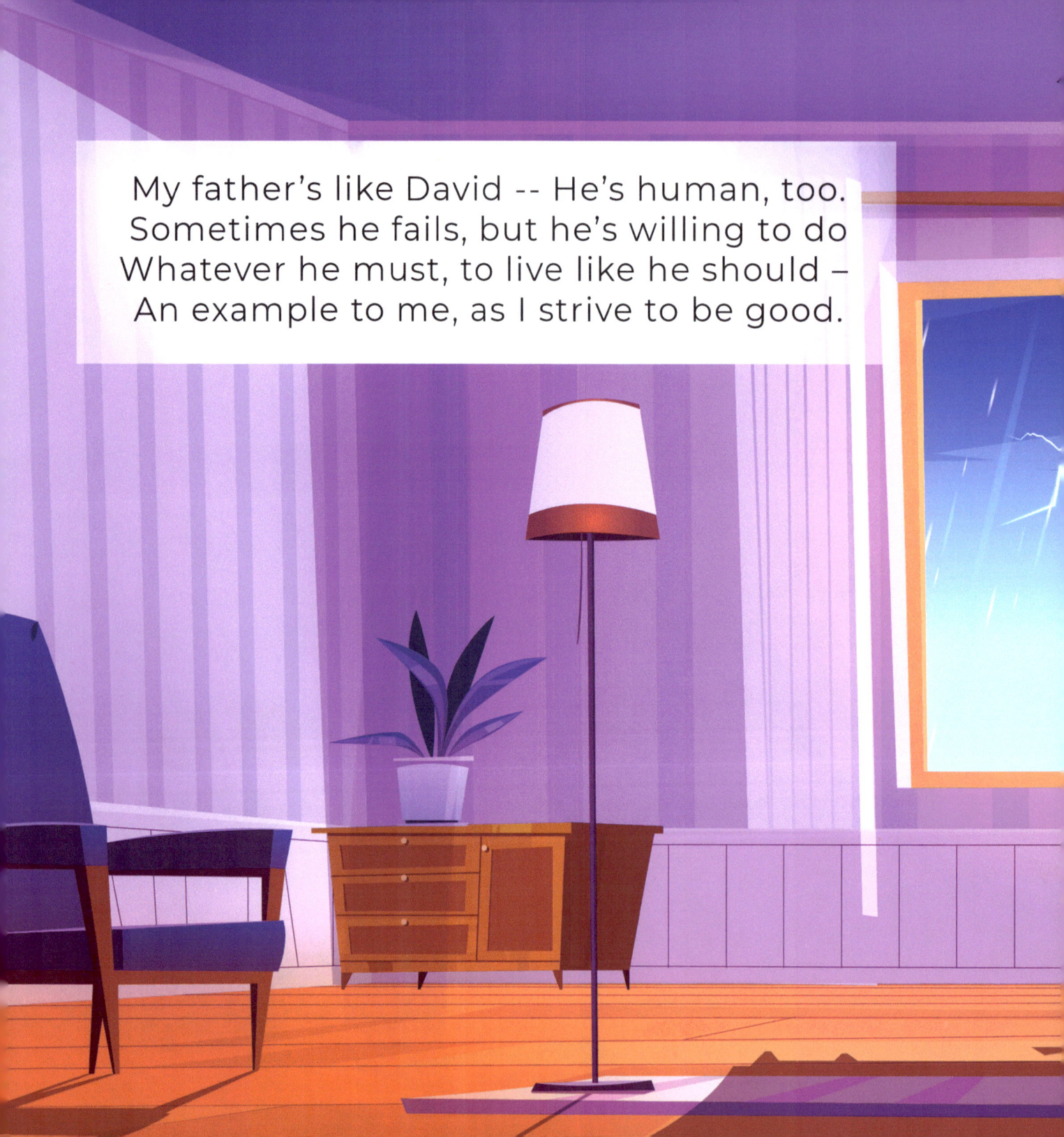

My father's like David -- He's human, too.
Sometimes he fails, but he's willing to do
Whatever he must, to live like he should –
An example to me, as I strive to be good.

David's son, SOLOMON, prayed to be wise
Instead of for riches, and so, in God's eyes,
Solomon found favor and God gave him more
Power, land, and money than he'd had before.
He also got wisdom, his first request,
For riches are good, but wisdom is best;

My dad is like Solomon; he always leads
Our family with wisdom and prays for our needs.

Do you know about DANIEL? A law was made
To worship the king, but he disobeyed
And continued to pray to the Lord up above.
Then the Lord gave to Daniel protection and love.

"Let the lions eat Daniel!" the bad king declared,
But the good Lord saved Daniel, and his life was spared.

Like Daniel, my dad worships God and not man;
No matter what happens, he follows God's plan.

Though He was God's Son, did you know Jesus had
A good man named JOSEPH for his earthly dad?
He worked as a carpenter; that's how he got paid
And cared for his family with money he made.

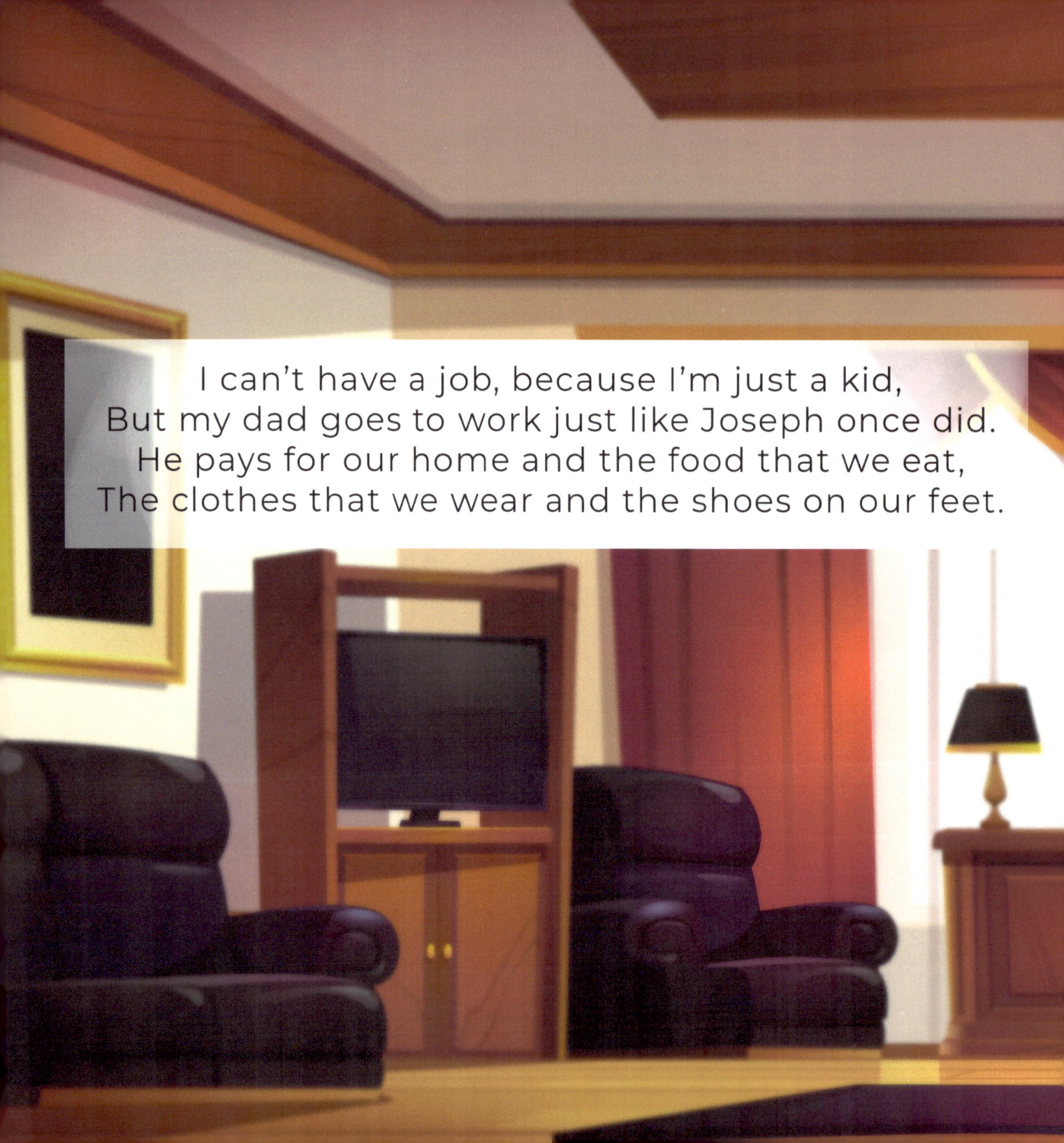

I can't have a job, because I'm just a kid,
But my dad goes to work just like Joseph once did.
He pays for our home and the food that we eat,
The clothes that we wear and the shoes on our feet.

Do you know about PETER? Well, let's take a look!
He once walked the footsteps that Jesus Christ took,
Even on water! – But it made him afraid –
Trying to follow the example Christ made.
Yes, Peter was there back when Christ's church began,
And he spread the Good News of Salvation to man.

My Dad loves the church and makes sure that I go
And learn from the Bible God's Truth I should know.

When we speak of Christ's church, don't forget about PAUL!
He traveled on journeys to preach Christ to all.
He also wrote letters to churches abroad
To encourage them all to stay faithful to God.
He was beaten, imprisoned, but Paul was someone
Who kept doing the work that he knew must be done.

My dad is like Paul, for he follows God's will;
If others don't like it, he follows Him still.

A young man named TIMOTHY worked by Paul's side
And strengthened the church by the help he supplied.

My dad is like Timothy; he's a good man,
Always looking for ways to help when he can.

JOHN taught God's children to love one another,
To treat those you meet like a sister or brother.

My dad is like John, for he freely shows
The love in his heart wherever he goes.

But the best man of all Who was perfect, we know
Was the Son of God, JESUS, and even though
My dad is not perfect, but with Jesus he is,
To be an example of Jesus to me.

Thank you, dear God, for the gift of my dad.
He's the best father a child ever had.
He's guided by Scripture, and walks in the Light,
And prays for me daily to raise me up right!

As a father has compassion on his children,
so the Lord has compassion on those who fear him;

Psalm 103v13 NIV

Author's note:

Thank you so much for reading this book. If you enjoyed this book, we would love it if you could leave a review or recommend it to a friend.

Thank you for your support!
Please checkout our other books

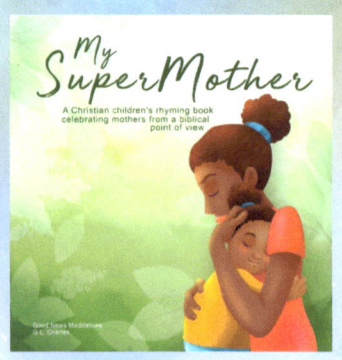

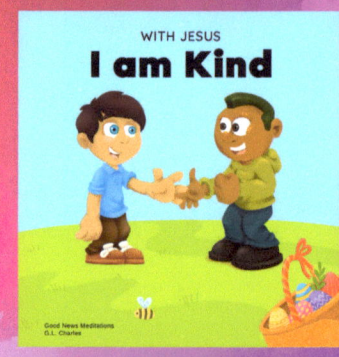

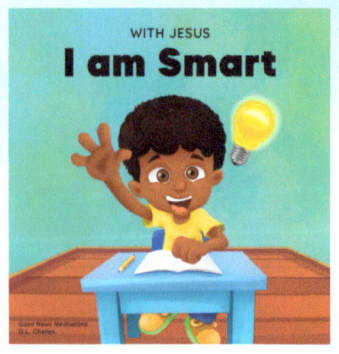

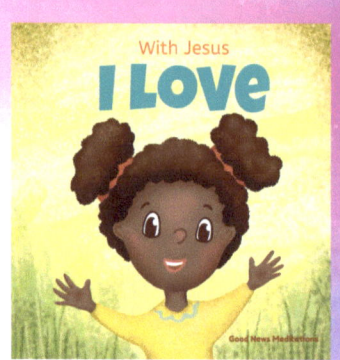
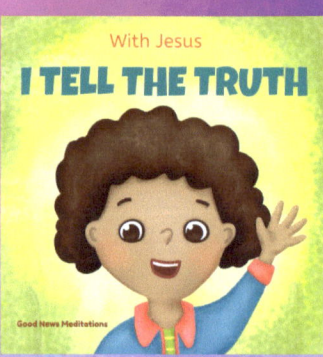

www.gnmkids.com

www.ingramcontent.com/pod-product-compliance
Lightning Source LLC
Chambersburg PA
CBHW041554120626
46551CB00002B/201